## What Families Were Like

# The Second World War

**Fiona Reynoldson**

based on an original text by
Nigel Smith

*HODDER*
*Wayland*

an imprint of Hodder Children's Books

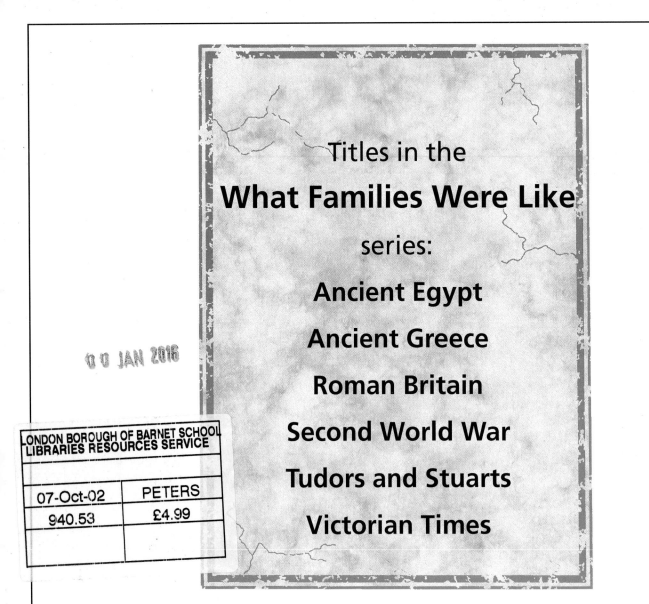

Titles in the
# What Families Were Like
series:

**Ancient Egypt**

**Ancient Greece**

**Roman Britain**

**Second World War**

**Tudors and Stuarts**

**Victorian Times**

**Designer:** Joyce Chester
**Consultant:** Norah Granger
**Editor:** Carron Brown
**Production controller:** Carol Stevens
**Picture researcher:** Liz Moore

First published in Great Britain in 1998 by
Wayland Publishers Ltd
This paperback edition published in 2002 by
Hodder Wayland, an imprint of Hodder Children's Books
338 Euston Road, London NW1 3BH
© Hodder Wayland 1998

**British Library Cataloguing in Publication Data**
Reynoldson, Fiona
Second World War. – (What families were like)
1. Family – Great Britain – History – 20th century – Juvenile
literature 2. World War, 1939–1945 – Social aspects –  Great
Britain – Juvenile literature 3. Great Britain – Social
conditions – 20th century – Juvenile literature
I. Title
306.8'5'0941'09044

ISBN 0 7502 4350 3

Typeset in England by Joyce Chester
Printed and bound in Italy by G. Canale C.S.p.A., Turin
Text based on *Family Life in the Second World War* by Nigel Smith
published in 1994 by Wayland Publishers Ltd.

**Picture acknowledgements:** Getty Images 8 (bottom), 9, 10
(bottom), 16 (top), 21, 23, 25 (top and bottom), 27 (top and bottom),
28 (left), 29; The Imperial War Museum 6, 7 (top), 8 (top), 11, 12
(top and bottom), 18, 19 (bottom), 28 (right); Kent Messenger
Group 10 (top); The London Transport Museum 15 (top); The
Newhaven Fort Collection *cover*, 7 (bottom), 13 (top and middle),
22 (bottom), 30 (bottom); Popperfoto *cover*, 4 (top), 5, 14, 16
(bottom), 17 (bottom), 19 (top), 20 (top), 24; Topham Picture
Source 17 (top). The commissioned pictures from the Newhaven
Fort collection were photographed by APM Studios. The
remaining pictures are from the Wayland Picture Library.

# Contents

# Saying goodbye

It was 3 September 1939. Britain went to war with Germany.

The war changed everything. Men had to go to fight.

So families said goodbye to fathers, brothers and husbands.

Many people were very upset. They did not know if they would ever meet each other again.

▲ A father says goodbye to his wife and baby.

Everyone thought the big cities would be bombed so children were sent to live with families in the countryside. ▶

Most men had to leave Britain and fight battles in other countries. However, some men did other jobs to help in the war. These were jobs such as coal mining and fire-fighting.

## Evacuation

The government thought the Germans would bomb the big cities. They decided to send all the children away from the cities. This was called evacuation.

These parents have come from the city to visit their children. ▼

They sent the children by train to live with families in the country. Each child took only what he or she could carry, such as a small bag of clothes and a gas mask.

CIVIL DEFENCE

# WOMEN WANTED FOR EVACUATION SERVICE

OFFER YOUR SERVICES
TO YOUR LOCAL COUNCIL

OR ANY BRANCH OF WOMEN'S VOLUNTARY SERVICES

NATIONAL
SERVICE

◄ Women in the country gave homes to evacuated children.

## Settling down

Many city children were sent to the country. They had to go to the local village school. It was difficult to settle down. They missed their families. They missed their friends. Everything was strange. Some city children had never seen cows or sheep.

## Far from the bombing

Some rich parents sent their children to the USA or Canada. They thought they would be safe. But sometimes German submarines sank the ships the children were travelling on.

Parents were told what to do when they visited their children. ▼

▲ This poster warns mothers not to bring children home.

### WHEN YOU VISIT YOUR CHILD IN THE COUNTRY

YOU CAN HELP the housewife with whom your child is billeted by making things as easy as possible for her during your visit. She will not expect to have to provide you with meals. You can give her a welcome rest if you take your child out for the day.

YOU CAN HELP by examining your child's clothes and boots and shoes in order to find out whether they need seeing to. You will naturally wish to do everything you can to keep your child properly clothed and shod. This is an opportunity for you to see for yourself whether anything is needed.

YOU CAN HELP by doing everything you can to encourage your child to stay in the country for safety's sake. DO NOT BRING YOUR CHILD HOME WITH YOU WHEN YOU RETURN.

## Evacuation again

Thousands of children went home in 1939 when no bombs came. A year later many bombs fell on the cities. But many families did not want to be split up again. So their children stayed at home while other children moved away again.

# Life goes on

Life was difficult for families during the war. Husbands and wives were separated. Many homes were destroyed by bombs. It was hard for women to look after the home on their own.

KEEP DEATH OFF THE ROAD
CARELESSNESS KILLS

◄ Many people died in car accidents during the blackout.

Families being apart upset everyone. Parents were frightened that their children would be hurt. Wives were frightened that their husbands would be killed. Soldiers worried that their homes might be bombed. Letters were often delayed. Everyone was worried.

▲ Men painting stripes on lampposts to help people see in the blackout.

◄ People enjoy a concert on a bomb site.

## The blackout

A blackout was set up. No street lights were allowed at night. Everyone had to cover their windows at night. No light could shine through. This was to stop German bombers seeing towns and cities. But people hated the blackout.

The edges of pavements were painted white to help people to see them at night.

Many people were killed in car accidents in the blackout. They also drowned by falling in rivers and ponds.

A bus has fallen into a crater after a bombing raid on London. ▼

These soldiers are checking people's identity cards. ▼

## Travel

The government asked people not to travel if they did not need to. ▼

Travelling was difficult. There was very little petrol for cars. Road signs were removed. This was to confuse the Germans if they invaded.

Many people rode bicycles. Families did not go on holiday.

The government said that transport for soldiers was very important. So there were fewer trains running for ordinary people to use. Also the Germans bombed railways in order to stop trains running. It was very hard for people to travel on the trains because they were so overcrowded.

Buses were overcrowded too. And driving in the blackout was very dangerous for the bus drivers.

IS YOUR JOURNEY REALLY NECESSARY?

TICKETS

IS YOUR JOURNEY REALLY NECESSARY?

BERT THOMAS

RAILWAY EXECUTIVE COMMITTEE

## Food rationing

During the war food and clothes were in short supply. The government set up rationing to make sure everyone got their fair share of food. People had to queue up outside shops for hours to buy food.

People did the best they could. They made cakes without eggs. They made coffee from dried acorns. Some people bought extra food on the black market.

▲ Shoppers waited in long queues to buy food.

Father Christmas asks people to give money to help fight the war. ▶

"TELL THEM TO MAKE IT A WAR SAVINGS CHRISTMAS!"

War Savings for Everyone!

## Clothing

Clothing was also rationed. New clothes were hard to get. People mended old clothes or cut up old coats or trousers to make children's clothes. Women even painted their legs with shoe polish when they could not buy stockings.

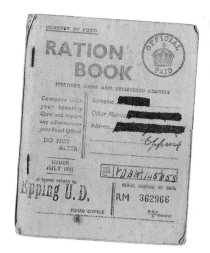

## Don't waste anything

People were told not to waste anything. They could not waste water. So they only had one bath a week.

People obeyed strict rules such as this to help win the war.

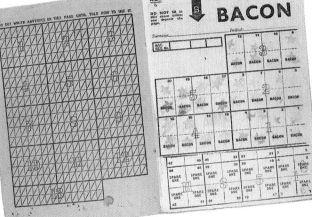

Everybody used ration books to buy food. ▶

| | Food rationing | | | | | | |
| --- | --- | --- | --- | --- | --- | --- | --- |
| | One week's ration allowance for one person: | | | | | | |
| One egg | Margarine (2 oz) | Cooking fat (2 oz) | Tea (2 oz) | Sugar (8 oz) | Cheese (1 oz) | Bacon and ham (4 oz) | Meat (Value of 1 shilling 2d) |

# The Blitz

In 1940, the German leader, Adolf Hitler, ordered the German air force to bomb London and other big cities. Hitler hoped the bombs would make Britain surrender. This was called the Blitz.

Many families slept in Anderson shelters during the night. ▼

## Air raid shelters

People were warned that the German aeroplanes were coming by wailing sirens. They ran to air raid shelters. Some families built Anderson shelters in their gardens.

## Underground shelters

Many families went to crowded public shelters. Night after night German planes bombed London. Thousands of people sheltered in the London Underground stations.

Signs were put up at the Underground stations. ▼

The platforms were crammed with people. It was noisy and smelly. Buckets were used for toilets. It was cold too. People took all their valuable things to the shelters. This was in case their house was bombed in the night.

Some people sang songs to cheer everyone up. When the All Clear siren sounded in the morning, everyone went home.

Every night families slept on the platforms in London Underground stations. ▼

## SHELTERERS' BEDDING

The practice of shaking bedding over the platforms, tracks and in the subways is strictly forbidden

◄ These people have walked into the country to sleep for the night.

These children are sheltering in a trench and watching aeroplanes fighting overhead. ▼

## Night time

Some people walked into the countryside every night. They slept in the fields. Then every morning they went home. They hoped their homes had not been bombed during the night.

## The bombing

People dreaded the bombing. The noise of bombs going off every night was very frightening. Thousands of people were killed in the bombing. Two million people lost their homes. Whole streets of houses were flattened by bombs. In one night the centre of Coventry was destroyed.

## Helping out

People helped each other during the Blitz. They made friends in the shelters. When people's homes were bombed, neighbours took them into their own homes.

## Writing to loved ones

When wives wrote to their husbands who were away fighting, they tried to be cheerful. They did not write about the horrors of the bombing. But soldiers knew that Britain was being bombed. The bombing made everyone determined to win the war.

▲ This family is standing next to where a bomb landed.

These soldiers are looking for survivors in the rubble of a building destroyed by a bomb. ▼

# Women at war

This poster calls for women to work in the factories. ▼

Women played a very important part in the war.

Many men were away fighting, so women did their jobs. Nearly all women did some kind of war work.

## Factory workers

Women were needed to work in the factories. They helped build aeroplanes, tanks, ships and guns. These were skilled jobs. This was the first time many women had worked outside their homes.

WOMEN OF BRITAIN
COME INTO THE FACTORIES
ASK AT ANY EMPLOYMENT EXCHANGE FOR ADVICE AND FULL DETAILS

Many women were keen to help win the war. They liked earning their own money, too. They worked long hours and were paid less than men for the same jobs. But it was a start. After the war, many women were unhappy that they had to give their jobs back to the men. However, the war showed that women could do the same jobs as men.

Working women could not look after their children. They were looked after by a child minder or at a nursery.

▲ During the war women worked as bus conductors.

This painting shows a woman worker at a machine. ▶

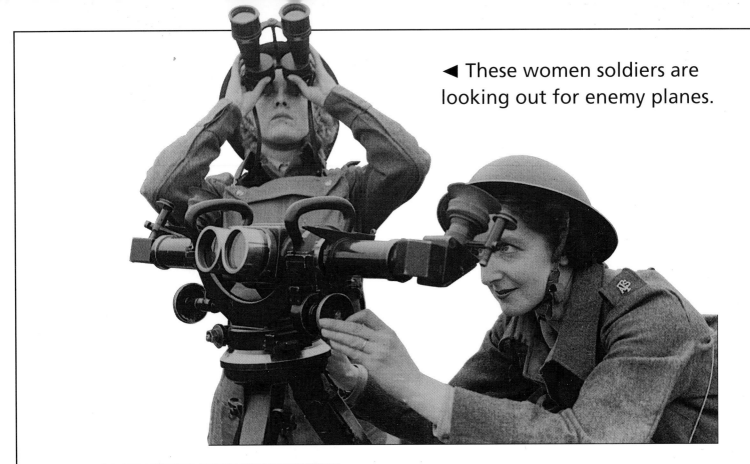

◄ These women soldiers are looking out for enemy planes.

JOIN THE
ATS
ASK FOR INFORMATION AT THE NEAREST EMPLOYMENT EXCHANGE OR AT ANY ARMY OR ATS RECRUITING CENTRE

◄ Thousands of young women joined the ATS or women's army.

## Women in the armed forces

Women without children often joined the army. They became army nurses and lorry drivers. They kept guard at look out posts.

In the air force women ran airfield control rooms. In the navy, they kept radio contact with ships.

## Other jobs for women

At home, women helped out during air raids. They took charge of air raid precautions. In the fire brigade, women rescued people from bombed buildings.

Some women joined the Land Army. They did farm work. They replaced men farm workers who had gone to fight. This made sure there was enough food for everyone to eat.

Many women joined the Women's Land Army to help grow food. ▼

# Children at war

Growing up during the war was hard. Sometimes it was dangerous and frightening. Children were frightened of the bombing. They hated being evacuated and separated from their families. They missed their fathers and brothers who were away fighting. Some children became orphans, because both their parents were killed.

▲ Children in this school class are practising wearing gas masks.

▲ Everyone had to carry a gas mask in case German planes dropped poison gas.

Schools carried on during the war. But there were often air raid drills. The children had to leave the class and go to a shelter. They also had to wear their gas masks. This was in case the German planes dropped poison gas.

▲ These GIs are giving sweets to the children around them.

## GIs

When the USA joined in the war, many American soldiers came to Britain. They were called GIs. British families made the GIs welcome. Children liked the Americans because they gave them goods from America such as sweets and chocolates.

## Entertainment

People stayed at home in the evenings because of the blackout. For entertainment people listened to the radio. Children loved to listen to Children's Hour every evening. This comforted children who were missing their families.

## Christmas

During the war Christmas was very different to other times. Families were separated. Children could not celebrate with their parents. People thought of loved ones far away. They remembered the good times before the war.

People listened to the radio to hear news about the war and for entertainment. ▼

◄ Christmas shoppers stand on sandbags to look at toys in a shop window.

Father Christmas delivers toys to children from a tank at an American army camp. ▼

At Christmas the shops were nearly empty. On Christmas morning children received very few presents. Sweets were rationed.

But people still put up Christmas decorations at home and in the air raid shelters. Everyone tried to have fun.

# Working for victory

This poster reminded people what they were fighting for. ▼

## Cogs

Everyone wanted to help win the war. Children joined Cogs. They collected rubbish such as scrap metal and old saucepans. The metal was melted down to make aeroplanes. Waste paper was collected to make leaflets and posters. Nothing was wasted.

## Scouts and guides

Boy scouts and girl guides did very useful jobs. They kept watch for fires during bombing raids. They helped in hospitals. Both girls and boys knitted socks and gloves for soldiers.

Boys joined the messenger service. They rode bicycles and carried messages for the army. During bombing raids they cycled with urgent messages to get help.

These schoolboys are knitting scarves for soldiers. ▼

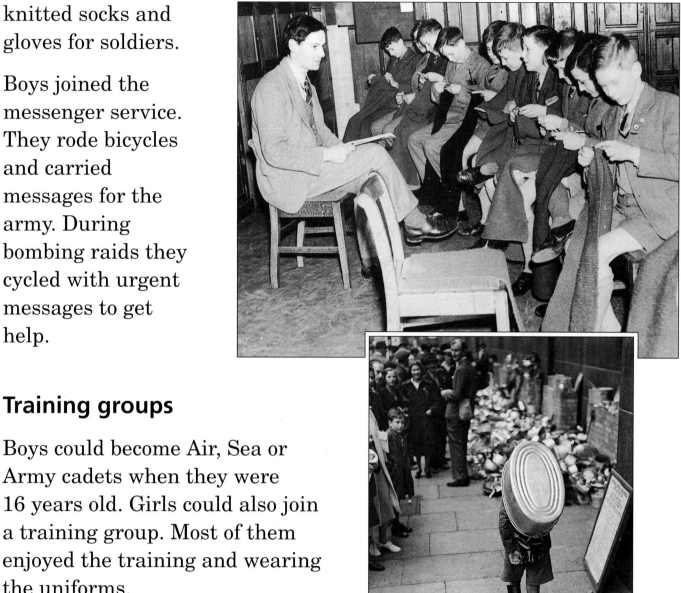

## Training groups

Boys could become Air, Sea or Army cadets when they were 16 years old. Girls could also join a training group. Most of them enjoyed the training and wearing the uniforms.

This boy is taking a metal bath to a salvage dump to be melted down to make guns and aeroplanes. ▶

Young people spent holidays and spare time helping on farms. ▶

▲ A sailor meeting up with his girlfriend at the end of the war.

HOLIDAYS...
HARVEST DAYS...
HAPPY DAYS...

BRING IN THE VICTORY HARVESTS

OCTOBER ••• MID-AUGUST & SEPTEMBER ••• END JULY-EARLY AUG

of POTATOES • GRAIN • FRUIT

ISSUED BY THE SCOTTISH EDUCATION DEPARTMENT & THE DEPARTMENT OF AGRICULTURE FOR SCOTLAND .......

## Growing food

Working on the land was very important. People needed food. Families turned their gardens into vegetable patches. Even school playing fields were dug up to grow vegetables.

## The end of the war

After nearly six years, the war finally ended. The men and women in the army started to come home.

They found many towns and cities had been bombed. Many families had lost loved ones. Sometimes it was difficult for husbands and wives to get to know each other again.

Thousands of women married GIs and went to live in the USA.

The people who survived the war were lucky. But everyone's lives had been changed.

A soldier returns home to meet his excited family. ▼

# Glossary

**Anderson shelters** Small bomb shelters made of corrugated iron covered with earth. People had them in the garden.

**ATS (Auxiliary Territorial Service)** Part of the army.

**Blackout** No lights were allowed outside at night. All windows had to be covered with heavy curtains. No one was even allowed to strike a match out of doors at night.

**Black market** Most food was rationed. People were not allowed to buy a lot of food. The black market was illegal. It meant buying more food than you were allowed.

**Blitz** Short for Blitzkrieg which means lightning war. People called the bombing of British cities the Blitz.

**Bombsite** Where a bomb had fallen.

**Evacuation** Moving people away from dangerous places.

**GI** Short for government issue. It was the name given to all American soldiers.

**Identity cards** These had to be carried by everyone to show they were not enemy spies.

**Rationing** People could only buy small amounts of food. They had to give the shopkeeper special tokens when they bought food. These tokens were kept in a ration book.

**Salvage dump** A place where useful metal items such as baths and pots were taken to be melted down and recycled.

## Books to read

*The Blitz* by Pat Kendell (Wayland, 1998)
*Britain at War 1939–45* by Michael Rawcliffe (B. T. Batsford, 1992)
*Evacuation* by Margaret Stephen (Wayland, 1998)
*Scotland in World War II* by Richard Dargie (Wayland, 1997)

## Places to visit

The places listed below are a very small selection of museums that have displays about life during the Second World War. Your local museum might have exhibits about life during the war in your town.

D-Day Museum, Clarence Esplanade, Southsea, Hampshire PO5 3NT. Sounds, images and objects are used to recreate scenes of life in wartime Britain.

Imperial War Museum, Lambeth Road, London SE1 6HZ. The most important war museum, with displays that include life in wartime Britain.

**Use this book for teaching literacy**

This book can help you in the literacy hour in the following ways:

 Children can use the book's contents page, page numbers, headings, captions and index to locate a particular piece of information.

 They can use the glossary to reinforce their alphabetic knowledge and extend their vocabulary.

 They can compare this book with fictional stories about the Second World War to show how similar information can be presented in different ways.

 Children can be made aware of examples of persuasive writing used during the war, such as posters.

# Index

Numbers in **bold** refer to pictures as well as text.